The Success Chronicles:
Real Estate Edition

The Success Chronicles
1.Business 2. Real Estate

ISBN-10: 1535190027
ISBN-13: 978-1535190022
BUSINESS & ECONOMICS: Real Estate

Special Dedication

To the many inspired, committed and focused real estate agents and brokers who have a vision, message, and a clear purpose this book is dedicated to you. The pages were written with you in mind to provide you new perspectives, new approaches and new ways of looking at how you can continue on your entrepreneurial journey.

Thank you to the authors in this book that shared from your heart, your experience and from where you are today. Without your words on these pages, many would not know the blessing it is to be a real estate agent and/or broker.

.

Table of Contents

The Success Chronicles: Real Estate Edition

First, to understand the journey, the lessons, hurdles, thought processes, disappointments, triumphs that you go through when building your career and business. Why is it important to learn about other's stories? Although the world is full of people often times when you are building a career and business you feel alone and at times you feel you are the only one experiencing the obstacles you face. Hearing and reading the stories of women that you can relate to, can empower you to look at your journey differently.

Second, The Success Chronicles is designed to help you craft your career and business in a way that distinguishes you effectively and memorably in your market.

Your audience wants to know how you started your business. How you came to be where you are at this very moment. They want to know what you like to do when you're not pounding the pavement with your brilliant work. They want to know about your path --- they want to know the person behind the brand. Then there's a really good chance they are going to trust you with their money.

Each of these authors share their obstacles, victories, and offer invaluable information that can help you grow, challenge yourself and look at your situations in a new light. I encourage you to learn from their stories and the lessons they have learned along the way to becoming successful entrepreneurs and professionals.

To Your Impact and Success!

BETSY FERGUSON

Founder, Lynchburg's Finest Real Estate

Theodore Roosevelt said "comparison is the thief of joy". Real Estate is certainly one of the more competitive businesses to be in. Combine that with the high drive and dominate sales personalities of the agents and the result over time can be a toxic concoction that kills the love you have for yourself.

I have been in real estate for nearly eight years now. I did not go looking for real estate as a career path. The path I was on propelled me here. I saw real estate as an opportunity to better myself financially. But I didn't realize, if I wasn't careful, how much and how quickly it could change me just by matter of association. How do you keep yourself from being tainted by the toxic pond you submerge yourself in on a daily basis in this business? Unfortunately, it is not just one simple answer. I will attempt to share with you some things I have learned that I think will help you rise above the toxicity.

Before pursuing a career in real estate I challenge you to define what success means to you. Don't just come up with an answer in your head. Write it down. If you don't, you'll end up never feeling satisfied or proud of yourself, because someone will always have a bigger victory than you. So if you define success as closing 12 houses a year, and you succeed at closing 12 houses a year, then you win! And when you find out your friend in the business closed 50 houses, you don't have to compare yourself to them-- you can celebrate them because you both succeeded. Imagine driving a race car but constantly looking at the lanes to your right and your left. If you do that it is going to slow you down. Perhaps even distract you from your goal. Keep your eye on the goal because the only person you are competing against is yourself.

So many times we get on Facebook, Instagram, or engage in a simple conversation; anywhere that someone can show you the best things of their life. Be careful, comparison can catch you off guard. I can be having a great day and then after scrolling through my newsfeed or having a conversation with someone, all of a sudden I feel like I have lost the wind in my sails. I start thinking about where I want to be instead of being content with where I am. I recently had a fellow agent in the business approach me and begin comparing our businesses, models and practices. It really affected my spirit for days after the conversation. Listen when I tell you that your journey is your own, specially tailored for you and no one can take that from you. When you find yourself comparing and looking at what other people have, you will find yourself subconsciously devaluing what you have. What you really have is something pretty special. It's special because it is specifically for you at this place and point in time of your life. I wish I could go back and tell my peer the importance of celebrating our diversity instead of comparing. Comparison requires someone be labeled the winner and someone the loser. Instead of her viewing me as her competitor why don't we choose to support one another and stand together as allies? I know how hard my fellow peers work to stay and be in this business and for that I respect them.

So if we know comparison is the thief of joy then why can't we stop? Social comparison is an innate human tendency. I have seen it time and time again with peers in my field. I entered this business in my early twenties. I am now approaching thirty and for the last couple of years I have gotten backlash from fellow agents in the business. Many of them have been in the business 15-20 years. They have dutifully climbed the ladder, steadily earning higher rankings. They were fine with this- until, a young girl in her 20's began growing her business at a high level and surpassing their early numbers. Numbers that had taken other agents a decade to earn. In an article published by CNN in the Fall of 2015, Schweitzer says we are hard wired for comparison and can't get away from it. The reason he says we are doing it is to make sense of our world. Do I make enough money? Do I need to update my kitchen? Do I need a new car? Are my kids doing well? Schweitzer says it's almost impossible to make those assessments objectively. So instead we turn to comparisons.

It was important to me when I entered my local real estate market as a newer agent to be disruptive. I did not want to do things the way everyone else in my area had always been doing them. I pushed the bar when it came to my social media presence. Both with my personal and business pages. I quickly realized strategic marketing would also set me apart and would be a reason why sellers would choose to work with me over other agents. I never wanted to run my business like anyone else's. I recognized early on that my differences were what made me unique and would be what made my business stand apart. My bachelor's degree in interior design, lighting expertise, kitchen design, development and new construction background could not be touched by anyone. No one else had the same make up and experiences I had. My business was never supposed to look like anyone else's, because it was unique and my personal journey.

Another thing to be on the lookout for around the corner of comparison is jealousy. Jealousy is often comparisons partner in crime. Comparison tends to foster competition over community. It also leads to feelings of inadequacy. The bystanders that only see the finale are usually those who are jealous. Jealousy has a way of focusing on only one thing. Jealousy doesn't give a complete picture. It ignores the hours of work that generated the sales and rankings-- the sacrifice of the time that could have been spent with family. Jealousy tends to overlook the years of practice, turmoil, confusion, and failure that preceded the success. Success always comes at a cost and jealousy tends to discount that cost.

We tend to as humans judge one another by the chapter of their lives we walked in on. Every life has its relative seasons of famine and bounty. Just because you walked in on a season of bounty doesn't mean the individual's life has always been that way. More likely than not, you are seeing the fruit of their labor from their earlier seasons of famine.

I spent my childhood and growing up years in Vermont. Many in the south refer to us northerners as "damn Yankees". Again comparison creeps in. I value my heritage, my northern roots because it molded me into who I am today as an adult. Being raised in the north though doesn't make me any greater than someone from the south. However, this is my perception of the difference. Northeasterner natives are more direct, brusque, "no-nonsense" and come off as aggressive to southerners. Meanwhile southerners come across to northerners as friendly, "without being sincere" and you never really know what they think. My directness in running my business in the south hasn't always been well loved by many. I value honesty and I am a straight shooter to my core. You will always know where you stand with me. I have struggled with owning a business in the south and constantly feeling like I am being compared to others because I don't sugar coat and beat around the bush. I've been tempted at times to give in and give up my no-nonsense approach.

My northern roots are what inspire me every day though. I will not change just to fit in and fit the mold. See when we compare ourselves to one another we lose inspiration. The question of inspiration is really a larger question of what moves us. What moves me. I recently read a great article in Real Simple magazine. The author Megan Abbott said, "As the years go by, as we grow older, we bury parts of ourselves, don't we? The parts that make us vulnerable. That show us perhaps as we really are". It's those vulnerable parts that our clients need to see, that they want to see. They are in fact what make us human. Allowing our clients to feel connected to us. That is why comparison is the true thief of joy. We cut ourselves short, most importantly we cut our clients, family and friends short as well.

What I have found is woman to woman we are the hardest on one another. I shared with you earlier about a fellow agent in the business who felt the need to compare our businesses and give me unsolicited advice. If you hadn't guessed it already she is a woman. I have spoken with many women recently both in real estate and other businesses and the one experience commonly shared as they have endeavored to accomplish their goals is dealing with women who instead of supporting their success, compete with or sabotage them. Women often feel justified competing with other women for many reasons. I will share with you some of the most prevalent ones that some friends recently shared with me. This message is so powerful. Not only for ourselves it affects our children and grandchildren. If we can get this message and impart the wisdom into our own lives, we will be able to have amazing relationships with ourselves. It is only when you have an amazing relationship with yourself, bringing out the best in you, are you then able to bring out the best in your children.

Insecurity. The definition of insecurity is self-doubt, not confident or sure. I remember in the sixth grade I had a tightly knit group of female friends in elementary school. We were the starting five on the girls' basketball team. We felt important and exclusive. Four of the five of us had an early growth spurt. One day on the bus to a game I was chatting with the four girls I considered friends. After all, we were the dominant girl force in our little universe. As we were chatting I watched one of the girls examine my legs propped up on the seat in front of us. "Look", she said, innocently enough, "Betsy hasn't ever shaved her legs yet." And she was right. I remember coming home after that basketball game and insisting to my mother that I had to begin shaving my legs. I thought I needed to hold to their expectation of shaving my legs at the age of twelve.

That somehow their opinion of me was fact and the need to fit in was more important than if I was really ready. I felt stupid. Less than. I had to begin shaving now so they wouldn't keep pointing it out and making fun of me. Women compete, compare, undermine and undercut one another --at least that seems to be the dominating approach of how we relate to one another.

By shaving my legs soon after that encounter I was proving a point. I had a need to prove that I could fit in, by comparing with the other girls who had already begun shaving their legs. It seemed at the time like such a small thing but I truly wasn't ready yet. What I was truly longing for was a need to be accepted. I thought by shaving my legs they would accept me. Turns out they didn't truly have my best interest. Turns out they really wouldn't be lifelong friends. Turns out the starting five was made up in an effort for each one of us to feel important and exclusive. A fabricated friendship. We were only using one another to feel good about ourselves.

How many women do you know today who are using one another to feel important, exclusive and accepted? It is in fact an artificial friendship. There is nothing authentic, sincere or genuine about it. The reality is that women don't have to devalue other women to find value within themselves. When we are fully able to see that we each are unique beings, then we can understand why we don't have to prove how worthy we are by putting other women down. If you want to better yourself, it does not take tearing another woman down to do so. You are your own competition, so start there. We are worthy just as we are, and its time we all started to believe that.

A part of the "competition" between women is due to the fact that we've bought into the idea that there is some sort of "limited stock" that we're all trying to attain. Whether that's the ideal man, some perfect beauty standard, perfect mother award, or a checklist of accomplishments. Somewhere along the way we have been convinced that for one of us to have it, someone else needs to not have it. It ends up making women a threat to other women. We see it on a larger scale in celebrity culture all the time -- "Who wore it better?" etc. On a smaller scale we see it as we scroll through our social media newsfeeds. It is like we are always trying to one up each other. When we post the picture of the most Pintresty party, a perfect family photo or how skinny we look in an outfit. We are putting these perfect moments out for the world to see and which lead to manifest shaming other women, disempowering them as they walk away feeling outdone. Whether we are doing this consciously or subconsciously it is an issue of misplaced self-worth.

It's women's emotional intelligence and compassion that make us fantastic leaders. Women who compete successfully have a self-assured awareness, a positive self-image, self-direction, are assertive when they need to be, and are aware of their own strengths and the strengths of their colleagues. Here are some final thoughts to getting this "thief" under control. It boils down to embracing other women as allies, whether that's at a mother's group, with our friends, in the real estate community or within business in general. Women should be kinder and stop competing against each other. We forget to appreciate how far we've already come in the direction of our dreams and goals because we are always chasing and comparing. Comparison after all is the thief of joy.

I challenge you to spend some time today or within the coming days thinking about how fabulous you are and reminding yourself of a couple of your unique and special qualities. Don't pick the easy stuff. Dig deep and remind yourself of the good stuff that only you can bring to the table.

ABOUT BETSY FERGUSON

Introducing the Founder of Lynchburg's Finest Real Estate, Betsy Ferguson. Betsy has a reputation for excellence, and a thriving passion for her family and successful real estate team in Lynchburg, Virginia. Betsy received her Bachelors of Science in Interior Design from Liberty University in 2008. With a declining job market and a pile of student loan debt she had to get creative.

She landed a job with a local builder/developer. He quickly realized Betsy was highly driven and needed more financially. He encouraged her to obtain her Real Estate License. Betsy has now come full circle. Two years ago she paid off her nearly $100,000 in student loan debt and today she owns and runs her real estate team out of the building she worked in fresh out of college.

Betsy's warm and contagious personality is what sets her apart. Her greatest joy is her husband Matt and 3-year-old daughter Layla Grayce. You will quickly see within her that family and people are what matter most. There is no denying Betsy's dominant drive to always push for more and it's not just for the sake of money. Betsy sees the good and opportunity that money can do for others. She is passionate about seeing her team members experience financial freedom and grow their wealth for their family's and future.

Contact:
- Website: www.lynchburgsfinest.com
- Facebook: www.facebook.com/BetsyFergusonInc
- Instagram: /www.instagram.com/thebetsyferguson

SHERRY SWIFT

President of Swift Transitions Inc.
Member & Partner with the
John Maxwell Team

Tell us about yourself and how you were first introduced to the real estate industry?

My name is Sherry Swift and I am the CEO of Swift Transitions, a coaching and training company. I am a Certified Coach, Trainer, and Speaker that specializes in supporting the Real Estate industry. We build rock stars, teams, and brokerages that set big audacious goals that are uncomfortable and exceed them through partnership, coaching, and systems. We believe that all true opportunity becomes available when we begin to do the things that make us the most uncomfortable. The magic happens right outside of your comfort zone!

I began my relationship with real estate in 1999. I was interested in investing and at that time truly believed that I only needed access to the multi-list system for personal purchasing purposes. I soon discovered my passion for the real estate industry and realized it's unlimited opportunities for personal and professional growth, along with wealth building. For many years I operated successfully as an individual realtor representing buyers and sellers assisting them in realizing their real estate dream. Although I met and exceeded personal goals consistently, my true learning began when my coaching and training business launched!

For over 10 years I have worked with many brands and hundreds of realtors who believe they have what it takes to dominate this industry. Through my coaching and training journey I have discovered that good intention, without measured application, is the cause for the majority of sales related failure. For this reason, I am known as the velvet hammer, delivering the truth, and redirecting distraction back to focus on the very few things that really matter to your earning potential and desired success!

What are the marketing challenges you see real estate agents make when marketing themselves?

Consistency and patience is the conversation around this question. Consistency is the key! One mailing, one ad, one door knock, will not make the sky open up and rain buyers and sellers and you shouldn't expect that it will! Many real estate salespeople focus too many hours on content, color and calibration; when they should consider that a simple message, delivered more often, will get the greater result. You should be prepared to financially invest in your business for a full year before you expect a return on investment.

I can't even count the number of times that I have watched a sales person stop six months before the pay off because they are impatient with the process…only to begin a new process that takes them back to day one! Lean not into your own understanding! Ask those who have walked the path before you and create realistic expectations for return. One more thing, current photos are IMPORTANT! If the primary reason for branding our cards, websites and promotional items with our photo is to increase face recognition, let's use a photo that actually resembles who we are today.

What would you advice someone when it comes to using social media to marketing themselves?

Everything and everyone is online. This can be a gift from the Google gods or it can sink your career in one search, Facebook share, or Instagram photo. Be mindful my friends, you are now a public figure and you are asking for the business even when you are not formally asking for the business. Be conscious of your audience, social media won't attract everyone. Understand that there is a distinction between owned, earned, and high jacked social media presence. So, when dipping your toe into the social media spectrum, be aware that perception of your brand can be easily manipulated by dissatisfied customers and clients or "internet trolls". Before investing you should know that social media advertising does not have to be expensive, a good amount of it is actually free and if used correctly will outperform any paid advertising. If you haven't already, sign up for a social media class or hire a coach to help you with this opportunity. In the meantime, search yourself on every search engine (each search engine can generate different content) - because everyone else is!

What would you advise someone who is stuck finding new leads in a crowded market?

An intentional consistent pipe line filling is the key to a business of abundant leads! Every day you must do some form of lead generation in your business. Lead generation is defined as intentional action that puts you in front of people who can say yes or no. You are truly in the business of making contacts daily and you should create a minimum expectation of how many contacts you would like to make per day. As a result of making these contacts, we meet people who need our services (whether now or later) and as a result, we get the opportunity to sell homes. The market is only crowed for those who refuse to do the daily habit of lead generation and creating conversation! Create a daily habit, find someone to hold you accountable to it and separate from the anxiety of "not enough"!

What kind of content should someone use to attract these leads?

There is a distinct difference between marketing and prospecting. Prospecting is the act of intentional conversation with people who can say yes or no to your service. Once you accept and decide that you need to talk to and connect with people every day, you need to decide how, where and what to say. Whether you are using a dialer system to dial into a neighborhood where you just sold or listed a home or you are calling expired listings and/or for sale by owners, you will need a resource for the phone numbers.

Most dialer systems offer add-on options, that allow you to search neighborhoods, or individual numbers for lead generation purposes. You need vetted tools that will support the act of prospecting by providing contact information for your prospects. Once you have the contact information, you need script and dialogue that create a consultative conversation between you and your potential clients.

What advice would you give someone who is ready to take their business to the next level?

In order to immediately create a greater return from your business you should commit to mastering follow-up and database management. There is a statistic that states that eighty percent of the business is left on the table due to a lack of follow-up! Eighty percent!! Eighty percent that is lost because we didn't call back, didn't stay in touch, they didn't know where to find us.

So many of us in the real estate industry have a "right now" mentality. If you don't have a need right now, we are moving along! Most of us have good intentions…we plan to stay in touch, but our attention is distracted by our need for immediate income. For this very reason we are not developing long-term, referral worthy relationships. This is why we need a dependable, easy to manage, contact management system (CMS) that will strategically store our contacts, allow us to stay in contact, and follow-up as promised. Decide on a contact management system, put it in action, create reminders for all of your promises, and watch your production shoot up!

How do you maintain consistent cash flow and increase your sales year after year in an ever changing market?

Consistent cash flow is maintained through consistent lead generation, database building, drip campaigns, and contact management systems (CMS). Lead generation is the heart beat of our business! Committing to a minimum number of contacts daily and announcing our service to a new group of people insures that our exposure continues to expand. We've talked about the importance of building a database of contacts, this database is your business and produces consistent opportunity, no matter the market conditions. Build a database as big as possible and store it in your preferred contact management system. The person with the biggest database wins! It really is a numbers game.

Once you have those contacts stored in your preferred CMS, you are going to want to put them on a drip campaign of some sort. This is a systematic form of communication that reminds your connections that you are in the business of real estate and it happens without you needing to remember to remind them. We must accept that we are actually in the business of connecting with people and as a result of doing that well and regularly, we have the opportunity to sell a lot of real estate. There is no magic pill, only hard work, consistent effort, and great habits!

What are some of the most successful systems you have used to run your business successfully?

We have talked contact management systems, these are a must to organize, follow-up, and stay in-touch.

- One of the industry favorites is Top Producer.
- Create thorough check list that make every deal strategic and insures that each client has the same positive experience.
- Time-blocking is a must when you are working hard to follow a schedule that keeps you in your 20 percent focus.
- I love a good mind-map that allows you to organize your thoughts and business plan on paper and measure your progress.

Finally, I believe the most important system is to partner with a brokerage that offers coaching and training or hire your own business coach. The opportunity to remove the static and focus on the things that matter the most is invaluable. Find someone who you trust and hire a coach! This single action makes every other system that we could talk about possible.

What are the mistakes you have seen leaders make that stifle the growth of their team?

As your real estate career and business grows, you will reach a point where you need leverage and leverage comes through people. When you reach a point in your career that you are consistently closing a greater number of deals every month, you will begin to realize that your time is better spent making new connections as opposed to filling out paperwork. Find people who have a skill-set that is different than yours. So many hire people who they like or who they are drawn to on a personal level. This most often shows up when an independent agent is ready to hire an assistant and hires someone who they would hang out with, and that has the personality traits of a sales person. Then, this same agent is deeply disappointed when this assistant is unable to focus on paperwork, follow-through, and details because they would much rather socialize with everyone in the office. Of course this is the case, they are you reincarnated!

When coaching my clients through team building, we intentionally avoid this mistake by utilizing the DISC system (The Study of Human Behavior) to focus on natural and adaptive behavioral types in order to identify the *right* person for the job. We DISC each candidate and qualify them to the next conversation, saving time and frustration.

Another great mistake that I've seen team leaders make is to hire or partner with someone who is going to increase production without having an administrator in place to take on the paperwork. An administrator is always your best and first hire. Finally, the greatest mistake that I consistently coach newer clients through is building a team too soon. Hiring more people than your team can sustain and before your leadership skill-set is ready to support is detrimental to long-term team success. Leadership is a tremendous responsibility and you should have *your* house in order before you bring others into it. Study leadership; understand the job so that you can train to the job, don't pull the trigger before you are ready! People are a responsibility, make sure you and your business are ready and make sure they are the right fit for your team!

What resources would you recommend, based on your expertise, that every real estate agent should have?

Regarding resources, it is important not to invest too much too early. Lead with revenue! It all begins with your business plan. How much money do you want to net, how many listings and buyer side transactions do you need to get there? Early in your career your best resource is a tool that allows you to connect with other people and support your priority of lead generation. Plain and simple, phone numbers connected to communities that you are interested in farming. You will need a contact management system that will house your contacts and make easy work of staying in touch, follow-up, and building a referral based business.

Mind-set management is invaluable because all growth happens from the inside-out. Study mind-set, read a lot, listen to audio books, and script practice by those who have reached mastery in these areas. You have to become another person. A person who accepts that this career requires a tremendous amount of momentum and you only get there through consistency. Of course you need business cards, sign panels, listing and buyer presentations…but without a priority on connections, and understanding the importance of behaving like a business owner who is responsible for promoting your business at all times, all of the flashy tools, pretty marketing and snazzy promotion is pointless! Most importantly, surround yourself with talent and people who have accomplished what you want. It is difficult to grow into something that you've never been exposed to.

Share anything that you would like the readers to know about you and/or your business.

- **As an Educator, Coach, and Trainer**, I focus on developing professional skills and creating personal growth with an emphasis on wealth building.

- **As a Trainer**: I bring my energy, insight, systems and process to new associates. I teach them how success in the Real Estate industry is by design by teaching the habits and disciplines that every successful associate possess.

- **As a Coach**: I bring my experience, ability to listen, and focus on the careers of emerging associates. Watching their careers very carefully and systematically helping them reach the next level.

- **As a Servant Leader**: I understand the needs of Real Estate veterans, who are in need of guidance and tremendous support that they can trust. I listen to them, their plans, dreams and goals in order to help them develop a plan and hold them accountable to their own standards. I support them by leveraging various systems while helping them on their way to building a dynamic team designed to support their individual business.

I partner with brokerages to support realtors in realizing their personal and professional goals through business planning, coaching, and measuring professional and personal progress. I am certified in over 12 John Maxwell programs, and lead mastermind discussions focused on integrating personality types and the study of human behavior in the workplace and in personal relationships.

In addition, I offer transitional, life, and grief coaching for groups and individuals, as well as program development, brand customization and much more.

ABOUT SHERRY SWIFT

I move people through Coaching, Training, Speaking and Real Estate! As President of Swift Transitions Inc., my specialty is in supporting the real estate industry, offices, individuals and teams by writing and facilitating training and coaching programs that meet and exceed goals. I have a tremendous passion for consulting, writing and facilitating training programs that are customized to any organizations culture. I am a certified coach that leverages a partnership with The John Maxwell Team to provide organizational leadership coaching and training. I live with my wonderful family in Southeast Michigan. I am relentless in my pursuit of your dreams!

Services offered:

As a member and partner with the John Maxwell Team, I am proud to present quality material that supports individual goals, leadership goals and organizational leadership development. I am certified in over 15 John Maxwell Programs and enjoy every opportunity to pour into industry leaders and sharpen their leadership skills. I am also certified in the study of human behavior (DISC) and will customize a workshop for your organization that shines a light on personality profiles and how they impact our day to day productivity and profitability. Real estate team building coaching and consulting available.

Contact:
- Email: Sherry@sherryswift.com
- Phone – 248-719-2400
- Facebook - www.facebook.com/kwcoach

SYLVIA ANN SOLIZ
Founder, Sylvia Soliz & Associates

Tell us a little about yourself and how you were first introduced to the real estate industry?

I launched my real estate industry business in 2005 when I was 25 years old. I started when the market was on its way down. I only got my license because my mom pushed me to do so while attending the University of Houston. I figured selling a few houses would help pay for tuition. I never intended for real estate to be my main career and it wasn't for a very long time actually.

Right out of college I worked with my mom at her clinic full time, exercising my Science degree in nutrition and health. I did this for about 5 years and decided a salaried job wasn't for me. I had more to offer. I wanted freedom. During this time, some of my close friends were having success in their real estate careers. So I decided to jump in and become a full time agent. At this time, I had no recent knowledge in real estate so I knew I had to join a top company where the main focus was education and sales. I joined Keller Williams since that's where I saw my friends were having lots of success and was told Keller Williams excelled in education and sales. Joining a new real estate firm changed my whole outlook on real estate and my personal life. Working with them got me really excited to start making money! Immediately I knew this was the career for me!

What are the marketing challenges you see real estate agents make when marketing themselves?

The marketing challenges I see that agents make when marketing themselves is that they don't "give" something to the client. A client wants to talk to you when they see that you are useful and providing great information to them. For instance, when we knock on a door, I just don't say, "Hello, my name is Sylvia Soliz, and I'm the knowledgeable Realtor in your neighborhood. Here's my card in case you consider selling your house. Have a nice day." That doesn't help the client.

I actually come prepared with comps of homes that have sold in their neighborhood recently and show them what their house is actually worth right now. This is giving the client useful info that they can actually walk away with. Then they will consider you as the knowledgable Realtor in the neighborhood. Also, market yourself as a large real estate firm. Even if you are only one person with one assistant, why not give yourself a bigger name, John Smith Team International! This gives the perception to the client that you are bigger than an independent agent. Why not?! I guarantee, if you keep saying it out loud you will eventually be that big team. I will discuss affirmations at the end of this chapter.

What would you advise someone who is stuck finding new leads in a crowded market?

This is the era of social media. If you don't know how to use it, hire someone that does and blast your name and company everywhere. On every social media account you can think of. This can be time consuming which is why a lot of agents haven't really been using social media to its limit. However, it's the best form of advertising right now and better yet, it's free! There are many sites out there that cater to managing your social media accounts and posting real estate related material on your behalf. Constantly putting my name and company in front of friends and followers will not let them forget about me when it comes to helping with their real estate needs.

What would you advise someone who is stuck finding new leads?

Go back to the basics. Door knocking and picking up the telephone and calling people. Consumers want to know there is a real life person willing and ready to help them. Consumers want to feel that they are working with an honest and caring person that will care for their needs. This among anything will beat out the mass emails they probably get daily from agents trying to solicit their business. If farming is something you've been itching to do, but believe that it may be too costly at this time, a very successful agent once said, "Why must one feel that they have to farm an entire neighborhood? Why not take one street at a time, even if it only has 5 houses on it, and keep marketing to them. You will look like the neighborhood expert to them since you are constantly in front of their face. Give whatever you do, 100%." So if you only market to 1 street, then you're giving that one street 100%.

What advice would you give someone who is ready to take their business to the next level?

First of all make it a full time job if you already haven't done so. Next get an assistant. A good one. Hire smartly. They will probably not be your "best friend" type of person. Probably just your opposite. You need someone that will organize you and keep your affairs in order. Once you start to receive more leads then you can start a team. For now, all of my agents are on their own except when I personally give them leads; then they are on a different commission split. They like this since they have the option of generating their own business as well as receive plenty of leads from me.

One agent serves as my personal showing assistant which gives him even more opportunity to make money. I have also made it a point to make my team multilingual to service a more diverse clientele. We service, English, Spanish, Vietnamese, and Filipino speaking clients! Every one of my agents also has access to my assistant if need be. I use a virtual assistant and this has really helped to keep my costs down. I will be getting a second virtual assistant to solely generate leads.

Also, don't be afraid of commercial real estate! I used to refer commercial clients out, but my love Joe, taught me commercial basics in a 30 minute ride to a Rockets basketball game and the next day I landed my first commercial listing (owned by attorneys)!

How do you maintain consistent cash flow and increase your sales year after year in an ever changing market?

I am so blessed to receive calls daily and my company must continue to help every one of them so I continue to grow my team since I cannot personally do it on my own. I make sure that my team have good training and live up to my company standards. My clients expect for me to be hands on, knowledgable, honest, and to fight for them. Therefore, my agents have to do the same for them. I am strict even with the agents that are my family. Business is business and they have to know that they will be held to the same standards as all the other agents on my team. People respect me for this and know that they will succeed if they follow my model. Aside from keeping my team motivated and on point with all clients, I also market heavily. But not marketing on paper (since no one really reads paper anymore) we market primarily online. We utilize most of the free advertising that is provided to us! Zillow for instance, has been very good to me on the free side of it more so than the paid side. People rely heavily on reviews. I try to get as many reviews as I can from my clients on Zillow. I've noticed that increasing my reviews and keeping my profile active has really increased my sales.

We all know clients are now doing their own leg work and finding their own properties online and only contacting you when they absolutely need you. That is why you have to be constantly in their face. Always remind them that you are there to help. Always pick up the phone, email, and text. Don't let them forget about you. You cannot be shy in this business. I accept friend requests from clients on social media and provide info through those channels that are useful and helpful to them. I speak to everyone and anyone I meet and ask for their business. Most people will tell you they are in real estate. But have they ever directly ASKED for your business? That is the key.

What are some of the most successful systems you have used to run your business successfully?

Almost everything I use is online based including my assistant. This keeps overhead very low. My greatest feat was getting my database organized and using a CRM. I was finally able to keep in touch with my clients on a consistent basis. We now send out monthly newsletters, cards, useful information, fun stuff through either snail mail or email. I've started hearing back from clients from over 10 years back! I wasn't able to do this before but I must say that something as simple as getting your contacts in order on a database is my most successful system.

What are the mistakes you have seen leaders make that stifle the growth of their teams?

Greed. I think a lot of leaders don't give back enough to their agents which causes low ambition and low motivation which then leads to turnaround and no loyalty. Agents want to be taken care of and to make money. Take good care of your agents, and they will in turn, take good care of you.

What resources would you recommend, based on your expertise, that every real estate agent should have?

Spirituality, Family, Business. In that order. I was working 16 hour days when I got back into the business having put business first amongst all things. I learned how important it was to put God first in your life. Have faith and believe that Jehovah God will guide you to success with all aspects of your life and then all will fall into place. Having a strong spiritual connection with God, then opened up my personal life to finally find the love of my life, Joe Rothchild. I no longer work during family hours. I feel this has really increased my work ethic and made me stronger in my profession. As for the business side; education, scripts and a CRM are a must. No matter how much you think you know or how confident you are in business alway stay on top of the industry by educating yourself constantly. You also always want to stay on top of trends. Always attend conferences, meetings, online courses, anything and everything real estate related. Scripts are a no brainer. You have to sell your services better than the next agent. Learn and practice the best scripts that will capture the client. A CRM allows you to always put everyone that you come into contact with in your database and keep that database alive by staying in touch with them all constantly.

Share anything that you would like the readers to know about you and/or your business.

I have come a long way when I first started real estate. As of now, aside from real estate, I am venturing out to explore new business ideas. But in order to accomplish new ventures, you have to change your mind set. You have to believe that no matter what, you will succeed. Always Stay Positive! Say your affirmations, daily. Maximize your mind's potential! These are the affirmations my mom passed on to me, and they have helped me to another level and still rising!

- I am ALWAYS in the right place at the right time
- I expect the best and I get it NOW!
- I ALWAYS get everything that is for my HIGHEST good.
- EVERYTHING GOOD is coming to me EASILY and effortlessly
- I am DIVINELY GUIDED in all I do.
- I EXPECT life to give me what is best for me
- I DESERVE the BEST and it comes to me NOW!
- This is a RICH universe and there is plenty for us all.
- I now EAGERLY await my GREATEST good.
- I EXPECT good fortune every moment of my life
- I am OPEN to receive the ABUNDANT GOOD that GOD has for me.
- GOD is the source of all my GOOD, I look only to HIM for my supply
- I envision only that which is for my HIGHEST GOOD
- My HIGHEST GOOD is manifesting in my life right NOW.
- God's wealth is circulating in my life. His wealth flows to me in avalanches of abundance. All my needs, desires and goals are met instantaneously because I am one with God and GOD IS EVERYTHING.

I want to thank first and foremost God for blessing my family and I with such great health, happiness and wealth! My beloved, Joe Rothchild for support and a most amazing relationship, and my family for such great support through my years in real

ABOUT SYLIVA ANN SOLIZ

My name is Sylvia Ann Soliz and I've been in the real estate business for 11 years. I own, Real Estate Offices of Sylvia Soliz & Associates. My license is held by my broker, Ultima Real Estate in Dallas, of which I am currently in negotiations to open the first Houston office with them. I am in a relationship with one of the top mega agents in the world, Joe Rothchild, who also has taught me a thing or two about real estate!

Contact:
- Website: www.SylviaSellMyHouse.com
- Email: Sylvia@SylviaSellMyHouse.com
- Phone: 281-300-4887

SHAUNNA OVERMAN
Lead Agent of The Overman Group at Keller Williams Realty

Tell us a little about yourself and how you were first introduced to the real estate industry?

Have you ever heard the cliché "mother knows best?" That should be the story of how I got into real estate. My mother once told me I would be a great real estate agent, years before I went to college to pursue other options. As a college graduate facing a grim market in the winter of 2009 I was fortunate to find a full time position as a mortgage document specialist with a national lender. Unfortunately, all good things come to an end and prior to market recovery the company was forced to close the doors to my office. After spending a while deliberating what I wanted to do with my life I came across an advertisement for a real estate marketing position. Remembering my mother's words of wisdom, I reached out in hopes of gaining knowledge and having the potential to one day become a real estate agent myself. I worked diligently to understand the intricacies of the industry, I learned quickly and less than a year later I found myself pursuing my real estate license. I've never looked back, and truly feel fortunate to have found my calling in life.

What are the marketing challenges you see real estate agents make when marketing themselves?

In today's real estate market, it is imperative to be aware of the latest trends when it comes to marketing. One of the greatest challenges in real estate is leading with revenue where marketing is concerned. As a real estate agent, one strives to build their own brand, be top of mind for consumers, and be top of the industry when it comes to marketing seller clients' homes. While all of these things are imperative, marketing can be costly.

In addition, agents new and old are consistently exposed to new marketing tools, techniques, companies and trends to assist them with their marketing. It is difficult to start with your foot on the brakes, and yet it is a must for new and upcoming agents. It is possible to be competitive early on without spending tens of thousands of dollars on marketing. Prospecting is the technique that makes marketing affordable for those agents that must lead with revenue. We often see agents come and go in this industry, and for those agents who aren't exposed to the mindset of leading with revenue it is easy to give up before their careers get well off the ground due to the expenses of marketing.

What would you advise someone when it comes to using social media to marketing themselves?

Having a social media presence in any industry today is imperative for survival. As a millennial, I myself often turn to social media to weigh the legitimacy of companies, restaurants and service providers before reaching out to do business with them. In my opinion, it is more valuable to have a consistent presence on social media than it is to spend hundreds of dollars on building a following or leads without value to give back. It is no longer acceptable to simply advertise your business on social media. One should strive to be personable, responsive, and spark valuable interactions that build relationships with their followers and friends. In real estate we are always striving to build trust and becoming relatable on social media is a stepping stone for us. Personally, I have hired the assistance of a social media company to aid in making sure my brand is consistent on social media; however, I'm still very active on reaching out from my personal pages. It's all about being social after all.

What would you advise someone who is stuck finding new leads in a crowded market?

Get out there and build relationships! Start talking to everyone you know, and ask to talk to everyone they know. Talk with the top agents in your office and see if you can assist with their open houses, or if they have any overflow clients you can take on. Find a mentor. Working with a mentor, whether in your market or another, will give you the knowledge and confidence you need to really thrive in this industry. There is more than enough business for all great agents after all. The most important thing you can do is spend time working to grow your business, and undoubtedly it will grow in return.

What kind of you content should someone use to attract these leads?

To me, content is less important than consistency. Be consistent with your lead generation calls. Be consistent with your farming. Reach out to your friends and relatives on a regular basis to remind them that you are in real estate. Ask people for business! There have been countless times I've lost business, stopped to consider why, and realized I cannot obtain the business I never ask for. So when it comes to content, the most important thing is to ask for business. Who do you know that could use your help? Who needs to know that you are in real estate? Find the 'Chatty Cathy' in your life and talk to her every week - ask her who she knows that needs your help with real estate.

What advice would you give someone who is ready to take their business to the next level?

When I was ready to take my business to the next level I did two key things. First, I hired a real estate business coach. The second may seem simple, however, I asked myself where I wanted to go and I set goals. My goals are so large my family, my greatest supporters, are often my greatest critics. They do so lovingly, and yet I know my goals are big enough for me when they seem impossible to others. After two years in the industry it finally occurred to me that I own a real estate business - I am not simply a real estate agent. To some, that may seem trivial and yet to me it was groundbreaking. When you own a business you have the opportunity to grow it as large or small as you like, you truly control the destiny of that business and in turn your own. I truly believe those that can grow such a prosperous business have the responsibility to give back to others, whether it be through opportunities or charity. If you want to take your business to the next level do two things. First, hire a great coach because they will help you grow in ways you've never imagined personally and professionally. Then, make a plan and cast a vision for every intricacy your plan allows you to have and accomplish in life.

How do you maintain consist cash flow and increase your sales year after year in an ever changing market?

Always have your foot on your financial brake, and have a phone in your hand to keep your business growing. Every Sunday morning, I visit my goals and my finances. At any time, I can tell you where I am in relation to my goals for the year and any gaps or excesses in cash flow. When I fall off pace I know something has caused me to fall behind in lead generation. If you want to control the market, you must be consistently seeking out new business. When you do, regardless of the market, business will continue for you. Even in a turning market there is business to be had, this is why the greatest agents survive market crashes. To be one of the best, all you have to do is consistently work on your business. It doesn't hurt to educate yourself on market trends and to be prepared to dig your heels in and work when the market starts turning.

What are some of the most successful systems you have used to run your business successfully?

Systems are the key to building a successful business in real estate. Without systems I have failed many times over. It was imperative that I put systems in place for organization and efficiency. The most vital system in my business is a customer relationship manager (CRM). In my business our CRM is our life source as it is home to all of our database. The CRM organizes our follow up plan for each client, provides a daily follow up plan, and more. Having a CRM is essential to success in real estate. I am also an adamant Google user. My email, calendar, drive, and more are all synced with Google apps. My Google apps work very well together and are so efficient that I know exactly when I need to leave one appointment to get to the next. As a millennial, efficiency and technology were non-negotiables when starting my business. Systems allow you to build a business and document it along the way, allowing you to replicate it if you so desire.

What are the mistakes you have seen leaders make that stifle the growth of their teams?

In my journey to owning a six figure team I had the experience of working on two teams that failed to thrive. In reflecting on those experiences, they had two commonalities. Both teams failed to have strong systems in place. When a real estate team lacks systems, it really isn't a business or a team, it is simply a group of people working together. Strong systems give a team the business basics they need to thrive. Both teams also had leaders that didn't embrace the ambition of their team members to grow and better themselves and the teams. In order to be a great leader one must embrace and strive for growth. All too often leaders feel threatened when others want to grow, and this can significantly hinder their ability to have their businesses reach their full potential. When you have team members that want to grow, embrace them and know that you have the opportunity to grow your business with them. That is not to say that some team members won't outgrow the team, because undoubtedly there are those that do, but great leaders will endeavor to help others grow in order to grow themselves.

What resources would recommend, based on your expertise, that every real estate agent should have?

In my opinion every successful real estate agent should have four powerful resources in their business: a coach, a mentor, a CRM and a passion for helping others. A coach is essential to drive a successful agent to meet their true potential by stepping out of their comfort zone. Having a mentor provides a successful agent the opportunity to grow without recreating the wheel or feeling uncertain when questions come up, and they undoubtedly will. The CRM is a key component of lead generation and follow up which is essential to any real estate business. Finally, without a passion to help others being a real estate agent is not enough to grow an incredible real estate business. I am blessed with the opportunity to have all of these pieces to help me grow my business year after year, and I know I would not be where I am today without them.

ABOUT SHAUNNA OVERMAN

Shaunna Overman is the Lead Agent of The Overman Group at Keller Williams Realty, based out of Greensboro, NC. A graduate of Elon University and lifelong resident of the Triad, she currently resides in High Point with her husband Bryan and daughter Mattingly. In just three short years Shaunna has built a family centered business. Striving for team members to be busy, balanced and blessed in their careers and lives is her top priority. Mentoring outside agents is a passion that drives Shaunna to lead by example. Shaunna lives for her passions by creating a business centered on team members' strengths.

Contact:
- Email: shaunna.overman@gmail.com
- Facebook: www.facebook.com/shaunna.overman
- Phone: 336-618-7564

CHANTEL RAY
Founder, Chantel Ray Real Estate

Tell us a little about yourself and how you were first introduced to the real estate industry.

When I was young, my mom sold real estate. I would go on showing appointments with her and learned about it. It ended up not being the career for her and she decided to become a kindergarten teacher. I followed her footsteps in teaching and received my degree in teaching from Virginia Wesleyan. I taught math at Cox High School. I followed my calling to be a youth pastor and then children's pastor. The jobs that I had did not pay very much and I wanted to provide a better life for my family. At the time, I was trying to purchase a home. I was having a hard time getting in touch with agents. Only one out of three agents called me back, and it took her a week to get back to me! I was just driving through a neighborhood one day and there was a homeowner outside. I decided to stop and talk to her about the neighborhood. She had said that she was thinking of selling her home and showed it to me. It was the one! That is when I decided to give real estate a try and got my license. It was the best decision I have ever made!

This was also when I had determined that agents just are not available enough. My vision was to create a system where someone was always available to answer the phone Monday-Friday, between 8am-9pm. This has now expanded to seven days a week! I want to make sure that a client does not have the same experience that I did and gets a hold of an agent on their time. Not on the agents' time.

What are the marketing challenges you see real estate agents make when marketing themselves?

Potential clients want to know about what makes you different. There have been rumors that many people have heard that I have a master's degree in marketing from Harvard. I don't, and I have never taken one marketing class ever! Agents need to let potential clients know what they offer and guarantee. They may be an expert in a certain neighborhood, waterfront properties or with first time home buyers. We have a lot of marketing that I have found from different industries that are working for us.

There is a local flooring company that advertised that if you were not happy with the flooring that you chose, they would replace it for free. That is where our Love it or Leave it guarantee comes from. If someone buys a home from us and in the 1st 30days they are not happy with the home, we will list it for FREE! This insures that our agents will find the perfect home for our buyers. We also have our 33-day guarantee. This used to be a 90-day guarantee, but the market is so red hot right now that we are selling homes in 33 days! If we do not sell the home in 33 days, we will sell it for free! How can you beat those guarantees?

We also track the money that we spend on marketing. We have created our own real estate search engine to track the leads that come through there. We used to pay one of the big real estate search engines for leads, but we really had to dig into the numbers to find out what the leads actually cost us. We discovered that leads could cost in the hundreds of dollars each! With our own website, we know exactly how much each lead is costing us. We are also using a company called Call Source that creates a phone number for special promotions that we run. These phone numbers are forwarded to our main phone number and we can track how many call are coming in from that promotion. We can see immediately if the promotion is working or not,

What would you advise someone when it comes to using social media to marketing themselves?

You need to find out who your target audience is. Our target audience is sellers, so we typically market to people around the properties that we are selling. You can really narrow it down to whatever you want. It could be a specific area, to people who own their own home, age or price point. We also know that most people who purchase or sell properties with us are between the ages of 28-48. Of those people, 55% are women and 45% are men. They make up 80% of our sales and that is who we target our marketing towards.

What would you advise someone who is stuck finding new leads in a crowded market?

Find your niche! It could be that you are the condo queen, the leader in luxury, or you love working with the 55+ community. You could even become the Kempsville King! Kempsville is an area of Virginia Beach that has become highly desirable. If you live there, you know the area and what it has to offer. Buyers and sellers are looking for their agents to know all about the area that they want to live in. Whatever the niche is, become the expert at it!

What kind of content should someone use to attract these leads?

If you want to be the condo queen, you should get in contact with the condo communities and find out as much as you can about them. Know all the pros and cons to owning one. You should be able to answer all of your client's questions at the drop of the hat. Write a blog on condos and give out free information about them. You should be the one stop shop on condos!

What advice would you give someone who is ready to take their business to the next level?

You need to ask yourself, "What is holding me back?" One of my favorite shows is called The Profit. There was an episode where a business owner was a baker and made pies. He could not keep up with demand. It was discovered that the owner was using a standard size household oven. Once three commercial sized overs were installed, his business took off! The question is what is your standard size household oven? We implemented repeatable processes with systems for them. Many of our processes are in power points for everyone to see them and refer back to them. These fully help you commit to the process.

We have process in place for everything down to the office refrigerator. Too many people were bringing in food and leaving it in there for weeks at a time. Not only was it always full, but it smelled. Yuck!! We put together a system that every Friday the refrigerator is emptied. If there is something that you want to save, take it out before 4pm on Fridays.

Other processes include checklists such as the one for our brand new agents. We give examples of what photos are acceptable and which are not for business cards, how to have their email signature read as well as what the script should be on their voicemail. This insures consistency and a high level of expectation of our agents. I have personally not sold a home in 9 years! I have people say that they only want me to sell their home. What I have to say to them is "Would you want the owner of Outback cooking your steak? They may own the company, but they are not in the trenches everyday doing the job. I have so many things going on that I would not be able to give your listing the amount of time it deserves. I have placed processes in place with all of our agents so it is like having me as your agent, only better!" We use a website called UberConference where we do weekly 8 minute calls with our agents and staff. It calls everyone so no one forgets the meeting and you can do it from anywhere! We save money with advertising by using a pay for performance program. An example of this is that I gave a TV station $2,000 to do some advertising for the company. If the advertisement does not preform to the standards that it was promised, then we get out money back. This way we are not throwing money away on advertising that does not work. Itis all about working smarter and not harder!

How do you maintain consistent cash flow and increase sales year after year in an ever changing market?

We started outsourcing many of the items that are not in our core competency. We used to have a photographer on staff. We had to pay a salary, buy the equipment, and pay for maintenance and mileage on vehicles. We decide to hire a photographer on pay by appointment flat fee. We only pay for what we need. There are other systems we have put in place, such as a service that schedules all of our showings. This frees up our agent and staff's time to do other important duties. We try and automate as many systems as we can so we can concentrate on the clients and their needs! You also have to have a plan with the profit of your business. 10% should be donated to charity, 10% should be saved, and 10% should go back into the business. 70% of your profits should cover everything else. If you cannot cover your expenses with that, then you need to figure out a strict budget and stick to it.

What are some of the most successful systems you have used to run your business successfully?

We use Salesforce to manage all of our leads. This system keeps agents on track and keeps all of our clients updated on the process of their real estate transaction. If an agent does not keep up with the leads that are provided for them, then they are cut off of leads. This also provides great information on what leads sources are working and which ones are not. Not to mention that we can see at a glance what our volume of sales are and what the company will be making every month. It really does everything for us! We use commission sheets for out agents. We have a program that walk them though all of the numbers so they can see what exactly they will get paid on each individual property. This is used to be a manual procedure and there was always information missing and agents would get frustrated. Now it is quick and easy!

Brokermint is what we use to manage all of our listings and transactions. We have quick and easy access to all of the documents and timelines in which items are due. We can add all of the contact of a transaction track our sign inventory, lockboxes and even see where we are financially. Brokermint has been amazing in that they have really worked with us to make this system custom to our needs. It has really made everything quick and easy for agents as well as our administrative staff! We have also created an inside sales team that captures all of our leads that come in numerous ways. This was a learning process, but we now are fielding majority of the leads that we receive. This is how we do it:

1. We pass the leads directly to the inside sales team without an intermediate step or two. They nurture those leads first. Agents used to get the leads directly and were cherry picking leads and the best ones. This would leave a lot of leads not

being nurtured. It was like throwing the baby out with the bath water. Leads are now assigned to agents based on their experience level.

2. Our inside sales team is fully trained on our systems. At first, they were not trained properly and the leads were not being nurtured properly. We have tried to optimize what the inside sales team is doing to convert the leads.

3. We were not tracking our conversion rate, so we didn't really know how well out inside sales team and agents were converting leads. Everything is about the conversion rate. The better the rate the better the company as a whole is doing!

4. We had to keep nurturing a lead instead of giving up on it. If you try and contact a lead 11 times; you have over 90% chance that you will reach them. If you are only trying two or three times, you will more than likely not be able to convert that lead.

5. Generating leads can be expensive. It is not about the most leads for the lowest price, it is about the best conversion rate. Radio and TV ads are very expensive, but the conversion rate can be huge! We have been moving more of our marketing to an online effort. About 80% of our budget is online and about 20% is on TV and Radio. We do nothing with newspapers, print ads and mailers. There is very little return and they can be expensive.

6. Leads are about quality not quantity. Find your niche and go after it! We know ours are people between 28-48 with 55% female and 45% male.

7. We do not disqualify leads because they decide the leads too early in the sales cycle. The potential client may not be able to get prequalified for about 6 months, but we can keep in contact with them. They could be a client in the future.

What are the mistakes you have seen leaders make that stifle the growth of their teams?

There is this fantastic podcast about leadership that has this amazing quote, "Success breeds complacency, complacency breeds failure." We are always trying to make things better and update procedures or systems. When you depend on your current success you forget that things change all the time around us. You have to stay current on all aspects of your business. We also try to create a listening culture. The next great product or idea will not necessarily come from the current generation but from the future generation.

We have a mission and vision statement and we stick to them. They are the heartbeat of our company! We try to figure out new processes for issues that may come up. We discovered that one of the best ways to fix some of our issues is to use automated processes for some of our procedures. A great example is when an agent is not updating their leads. This is a requirement for all of our agents to keep all of the leads that we provide them updated. When they are not, our system takes them off the que to receive new leads. The agents respond to this better than someone having to tell them that they are not allowed to have leads. This also frees up time for our managing partners to work on other duties that they have.

What resources would you recommend, based on your expertise, that every real estate agent should have?

Implement systems that will help you and your business grow. We spent $100,000 to get to where we are now with Salesforce and really track all the ins and outs of our company. Brokermint keeps all of our transactions on track and organized. Not every agent or real estate company can spend the kind of money that we have, but there is a system for everyone on any kind of budget.

Share anything that you would like the readers to know about you and/ your business.

One of the best things about our company is our mission and vision statement. It really says who we are and what we believe!

Mission Statement:
To glorify God by putting our clients' interests above our own, providing the highest level of honesty and expertise before, during, and after each transaction.

Vision Statement:
To be the only TRUE real estate franchise that provides an EXCELLENT & CONSISTENT customer experience 100% of the time.

We base every decision on what's best for:
- 1st – Our clients
- 2nd – Our Company as a whole
- 3rd – Individual team members

We have also started a new donation program called CR Cares. CR Cares is a 501(c)(3) public charity created to support

Chantel Ray associates and their families with hardship as a result of a sudden emergency and the Hampton Roads community with a sudden emergency or hardship. Hardship is defined as a difficult circumstance that a person or family cannot handle without outside help. The charity is the heart of Chantel Ray Real estate culture in action –Our goal is 3 FOLD:

1) To help Chantel Ray Real Estate Associates and their immediate family with hardships with a result of a sudden emergency
2) To help LOCALS in Hampton Roads and their family with hardships as a result of a sudden emergency.
3) Helping local churches and charities that help people in need or helping them grow closer to God.

This gets our whole company involved in donating to helping others!

ABOUT CHANTEL RAY

I have been in the real estate business since 2004 and have grown Chantel Ray Real Estate into one of INC 500's fastest growing companies! We are working hard to become the first true franchise in real estate where a client can get the same great experience over and over again no matter where you live!

Chantel Ray Real Estate sells residential properties in the Hampton Roads are. Our mission statement is to glorify God buy putting the clients' interests above our own, providing the highest level of honesty and expertise before, during and after each transaction. We truly believe that our clients come first! We offer a 33-day guarantee on our listings or we will sell your house for free! If it has to sell, call Chantel!

Contact:
- Email: sales@chantelray.com
- Phone: 757-216-5790 or 757-216-5796

SARAH CHATEL

Realtor with Keller Williams

Member of KW Global Property Specialist

Tell us a little about yourself and how you were first introduced to the real estate industry?

I grew up in Sanford, Florida in the 1960s and 1970s. My father was our small town's banker and my mother a stay at home mom. Throughout my childhood, my parents' passion was buying and renovating historic homes in our small town. This was the primary way they built wealth for their retirement. My dad had a knack for picking houses with "great bones" and my mom had a flair for transforming the ordinary into the extraordinary. She knew how to make a home inviting and welcoming by using curb appeal and high end decorating ideas on a low budget. Our family spent a good deal of time in transforming these diamonds in the rough. It was only after beginning my real estate business that I truly understood the wisdom and insights I absorbed by watching my parents transform these houses into homes.

One of the things I am proud of is how mom single-handedly returned a long neglected downtown historic neighborhood back to its original beauty. She was well into her 60's by then and was determined to leave a legacy of beauty in our small town. She and dad bought, renovated and sold 4 historic properties during their later years. When everyone else her age was enjoying retirement she successfully added some of these homes to the National Register of Historic Places. Her love of old homes wasn't lost on me. I seem to have the same knack when I walk into a home that needs work. To me, it looks like a diamond in the rough and I get misty eyed thinking of the possibilities. "Leave a place better than you found it," was my mom's mantra and I have strived for and passed this on to my children as well.

What are the marketing challenges you see real estate agents make when marketing themselves?

The number one marketing challenge for real estate agents is differentiation. How does an agent distinguish themselves and/or their team from others in the industry to become the preferred partner for buyers, sellers and investors? After all, there are many great real estate agents from which people can choose! Questions to ask are: What makes my team and me different? What is our value proposition statement; ie: what specific services we will provide? How do you define your value proposition statement?

A great place to begin is with clarity around mission, vision, values, beliefs, perspectives and of course your BIG WHY. So many Realtors fail to define who they are and where they plan to be by not defining these critical aspects of themselves or their teams. At Keller Williams, we are taught that knowing, defining and articulating these things are at the heart and soul of a successful Real Estate agent and team. Throughout Gary Keller's The Millionaire Real Estate Agent, agents are challenged to strive to be the best person they can be by being clear on what their Big Why is as well as their mission and vision. The high achieving agents Keller interviewed for this book all agreed: Knowing these things about yourself gives you unlimited possibilities.

So how do you define and articulate your BIG WHY? Much has been discussed of late to describe what a Big Why is and how to go about defining your own. For me, I did coaching with Jack Canfield Coaching (Chicken Soup for the Soul), Michael Maher (7L – Seven Levels of Communication) and others, in hopes they'd tell me what my Big Why *should* be. I couldn't figure it out for the life of me. It was the most elusive thing I chased, finally discovering that it was within me all the time! Philanthropy was my passion. So why didn't I make that my Big Why? Additionally, at my Dad's funeral in 2005, most in attendance commented that he had left a legacy of love. Ultimately, I married the two and came up with my Big Why statement: To Leave a Legacy of Love by Donating a Million Dollars and Teaching Others to Do the Same.

What makes good mission and vision statements? A good mission and vision statement is concise and inspirational. They are each easy to memorize and repeat. They are clear, engaging, realistic, and describe a bright future. They should clearly state your intentions, reflect your values, and demonstrate your commitment to live these values.

A compelling *mission* statement needs to tell: what you do, who you serve, and why you do what you do.

Vision is what the world, marketplace, or lives look will look like after you've accomplished your mission. It answers the question, "What will your life, the lives of those around you and your community look like once the mission has been accomplished?"

Values are what is important to you. They are the principles you operate under to accomplish your mission and vision. It answers the question, "What is important to you?"

Beliefs are what you believe to be true. It answers the question, "What rules will you follow?"

Perspective is how you view yourself. It answers the question, "How do you view yourself or your business at this moment. Where is your business today?"

My personal mission statement is "To create opportunities for people to learn and grow through teaching, training, writing and mentoring in order for them to find their destiny and purpose."

My business' mission statement is "Positively impacting the lives of others through real estate."

My team has a separate mission statement. "The Distinctive Atlanta Homes (DAH) Team is dedicated to simplifying the business of real estate by leveraging our connections and insights with compassion and integrity in service to others."

My personal vision statement is "Continuing a life time of learning and growing as I seek my unlimited potential in order to leave a legacy of love for future generations."

My business vision statement is: Bold Intentional Growth. (BIG) Think Big. Act Big. Achieve Big.

My values are summed up with these key words: Integrity, Loyalty, Authenticity and Charity.

My business values are summed up with these key words: Loyalty, Prosperity, Charity, Teamwork, Integrity and Global View. We defined them as a team and you will find those definitions at the end of this chapter.

My personal beliefs are that "Thinking abundantly opens the infinite possibilities God and the Universe have to offer and a scarcity mindset shuts down those possibilities."

My business belief statement is "Working together collaboratively allows everyone to vastly exceed personal limitations."

My personal perspective is "At 58, I've entered the golden age of my life, finally able to tap the wisdom within me. Because I have had so many rich learning opportunities, it is my duty to share this wisdom with others through teaching, training, writing and mentoring in order to encourage them along their journey."

My business perspective is "We are a newly formed Real Estate team that benefits greatly and leverages the knowledge and wisdom of more experienced, high performing teams."

I'm providing these as only an example. My encouragement to you is to come up with your own statements of purpose and passion which will give you the focus and momentum to achieve things you never thought possible. It's never too late to live the life you always dreamed of! If you are interested in a workshop on discovering you mission, purpose or Big Why, send an email to: info@distinctiveatlantahomes.com. We'd love to schedule a workshop for your office or team.

What would you advise someone when it comes to using social media to marketing themselves?

Being in the age of social media, if you are not using it to market your real estate business, you are missing a huge opportunity! Twenty percent of my business comes from social media engagements. In terms of effectively using social media to market your real estate business there are five important things to remember: scan, focus, consistency, value, and appreciation.

Scan -- Success with social media and content marketing requires more scanning and less scribing. It is important to scan and read your target audience's online content and join discussions to learn what's important to them. Only then can you create content and spark conversations that add value rather than clutter to their lives.

Focus – Define your real estate business and the brand you are trying to create. Then follow a highly-focused social media and content marketing strategy which builds that brand organically. If you can afford to, hire someone to help you with this. Summer internships for college students who are majoring in Marketing can be good places to find talent. Remember, you can't be all things to all people, so stay focused on what you do best and tout that.

Consistency -- Social media and content marketing success doesn't happen overnight. If you publish amazing, quality content and work to build your online audience of quality followers, they'll share it with their own audiences on Twitter, Facebook, LinkedIn, Instagram, their own blogs and more. This sharing and discussing of your content opens new entry points for search engines like Google to find it in keyword searches (get familiar with Google analytics and utilize key words). Those entry points exponentially provide ways for people to find you online.

Value – Remember, you must add value to the social media conversation. "Provide value or vanish." Focus less on conversion and more on finding and creating valuable content and developing relationships with others online. In time, those people will become a powerful catalyst for word-of mouth marketing for your business. Coming from contribution is very powerful. People can see insincerity very easily on social media. Your value will be ultimately judged as to the level of contribution you have made to others.

Appreciation – "What you appreciate appreciates." A portion of your day could be time blocked to focus on sharing and talking about content published or posted by others. If you want others to share your content, you must first share and talk about them. Appreciating others' dogs, children, spouses, businesses, etc. will be reciprocated in due time. Pay sincere social media deposits to others by appreciating them and in turn they will appreciate you.

What would you advise someone who is stuck finding new leads in a crowded market?

If you are stuck and all else seems to be failing, remember to ask yourself three questions:

1. What are you passionate about?
2. What are your talents?
3. How can you offer value to others?

Let your passion guide you to new people and opportunities. Where can you volunteer your time? Offering value to people builds relationships which can result in direct or referred business. For example, early on in my career I hit an imaginary wall. I was stuck and depressed because business wasn't good. But because I'm a naturally happy person, depression didn't suit me for long. Using creative thought, I decided to offer 2 hours of free home staging and organization consultations on a community Facebook page in hopes that it would re-ignite positive energy within and around me. Within hours of posting my offering of time and talents, I had 10 women (all young and with small children at home) requesting my help. It was fun to go into their homes and help them without any expectation.

Besides helping me to reset my mindset to one of service, I was reminded of the concept of paying it forward. Many women helped me along the way when I, too, had small children at home.

What kind of social media content should someone use to attract these leads?

Well, I think I may have addressed this question in my responses above, but let me try to offer a few additional thoughts on how to attract leads. I suggest that you use an acronym that others use for goal setting – SMART. When you plan content make sure that it:

- **S**peaks to your reader and demonstrate an understanding of what your readers need. Your content must be relevant in order to be read.

- **M**akes your message enthusiastic by engaging the positive emotions of your readers. Make sure your message connects with the reader in a positive and uplifting manner. Find a way to pique your viewers' curiosity by sharing exciting information in your field. Don't be afraid to make creative or unusual connections from seemingly unrelated fields. Start with a strong headline and then clearly communicate how the information you are providing helps prospects solve their challenge.

- **A**dvances your value proposition with your content. Make sure your reader understands the benefits of doing business with your team and brand, and what sets your team and brand apart from the competitors. Your content should do more than engage your prospects. Ensure your content revolves around trading useful information like e-books, webinars, podcasts or checklists, for a lead. Your content should also persuade prospects to share their contact information in exchange for materials they find valuable.

- **R**esearches and builds relationships. Try a variety of content to see which formats get better responses. Most people visit the web to research, as well to purchase. Social proof, such as customer reviews on your social media or blog, will help establish expertise and credibility. No matter which channels you choose, be sure they include clear, accessible calls-to-action and contact options.

- **T**ransmits timely information that is current and useful to your readers. Current information has greater credibility. Ensure your content conveys recent studies, research finding, articles and insights in order to capture credibility with your readers.

What advice would you give someone who is ready to take their business to the next level?

The best way to take your business to the next level is to find others who have already achieved the successes that you want, and then, find a way to spend some time with them to understand how they have achieved these successes. Don't be afraid to ask if you could shadow them for a day. Be curious and ask them: "What adversities have you overcome? What mistakes have you made? What systems did you implement that made the biggest difference in growing your business? What is the one thing you would recommend doing first so I can move from where I am to where I want to be? What do you know now that you wish you knew then?"

For example, when I wanted to move my average sales price up to a luxury level, I asked a seasoned agent to co-list my friends' luxury home in exchange for mentoring during the process. I gave up 50% of my commission for 3 months of mentoring = priceless. Never be afraid to ask for help.

As soon as you are financially able, get a business / real estate coach. It is an invaluable investment for you personally and will pay unlimited dividends on current and future business. To borrow from Diana Kokoszka, CEO of Keller Williams MAPS Coaching, a coach will help you "create a life by design not by default." Said another way, you cannot expect to realize different results by practicing the same behaviors and following the same processes – you must change, you must improve, you must "raise your lid" in order to raise your performance or that of your team. The key is to figure out where you need to raise your lid as a leader or agent. Because we all have our blind-spots, it's hard for people to figure out personal or business limitations without the help of an unbiased third party. A mentor or coach can help push pass these limitations through feedback and/or coaching.

How do you maintain consistent cash flow and increase your sales year after year in an ever changing market?

In order to maintain consistent cash flow and increase your sales year over year, a commitment to consistent lead generation should be the cornerstone of your business. Make contact with at least 50 people each week. Reach out to people you know and don't know. Understand what is happening in their lives, where you might add value to them or share some new insights or experience. Come from contribution. You'll be top of mind when they think about Real Estate.

The top 20% of any market will tell you that they consistently call their database to stay in touch. Did you know your phone contains gold? Start with just the contacts in your phone and work to add from there. You will be well on your way to a prosperous Real Estate career. Gary Keller says in The Millionaire Real Estate Agent that the average ratio is 2:12 – 2 sales come from 12 contacts. If you have 100 people in your phone, and you called them, emailed and provided pertinent information to them, at the end of a year to 18 months you'd have 2 sales. What if you had 500 contacts in your phone or a contact management system? By adding at least 100 contacts per year for several years, you too could be a Millionaire Real Estate agent, if that is your goal. Add contacts to your database by joining civic organizations, churches or synagogues, PTA, sports, charitable organizations, etc. Stay in touch with them because people ultimately do business with people they know, like and trust.

Because I have lived in Atlanta for 38 years, I have over 3000 people in my database. My team and I make it our priority to stay in touch and provide content or information that they may find helpful, 33 times a year. Michael Maher, one of my real estate coaches told me years ago, "Lead with the giving hand." By consistently coming from contribution, providing helpful information and seeking to be of service, the percentages are stacked in my favor that when they consider any Real Estate transaction, they will think of me.

Another thing that will add consistency to your business and therefore your cash flow is to implement a system to stay in touch with your database. Without a system, it is difficult for even extraordinary people to produce ordinary results consistently. You must not only have systems; you must know what each system is yielding based on the results.

Keller Williams has a system called a 33 touch, which helps agents communicate with their database 33 times per year through emails, phone calls and mailing something of value. Our team sets up our 33 touch schedule in the fourth quarter for the coming year. It can change during the year based on new events or information which comes available. An effective communication campaign, such as a 33 touch, assures greater consistency with sales and cash flow. We also track the conversion rates. At the end of the year we determine which campaigns worked and which ones didn't in order to adjust our plan for the following year.

In terms of increasing sales, year over year, once you are consistent with lead generation and your communication system with your database, you can add an additional system to your business, if you have the leverage to support it. Paying for leads from Realtor.com or Zillow is controversial because you must not only have the people power to convert these leads as they come in and it can never replace picking up the phone to make lead generation calls.

A cost effective way to find leads is "farming" a local neighborhood, which takes approximately 18 months to see results. Farming consists of sending monthly postcards, door knocking with something of value as well as being seen regularly in your farm. If you do these things consistently for 18 months, you will then see a return on your investment of time and money.

However, anything you implement must be tracked in order to see conversion rates. Understanding the predictable results from each system will help you with business planning the following year. Additionally, to continue to increase sales year over year, you will have to add talent or leverage to your Real Estate team. This process will also add additional contacts which the new team members will bring with them.

Lauren, my Operations Manager, came to me at a time when I didn't think I could afford her. My husband, Peter Chatel, encouraged me to take that leap of faith and said, "talent doesn't come around all that often. Your business will expand with her expertise and she'll pay her salary back times three within the year." Thankfully I listened to him because she has been an amazing asset to my business as well as to me personally. She came on board with our team, needing no training – she actually had to train me, and was totally committed to our mission, vision, values, beliefs and perspectives.

But I have to tell you that going from a solo agent to a team felt like a hot air balloon that's on the ground. When the fire is lit and the balloon starts to rise, untethered, it's jerky until it gets above the clouds. After that it's a smooth ride, unless there's a storm on its way. But a good pilot (Team Leader) knows how to guide hot air balloons (and teams) through those turbulences. I know we will run into obstacles, because we are human and we are still learning and growing, but as long as we are committed to our systems, analytics and abundance mindset, the sky is the limit.

What are some of the most successful systems you have used to run your business successfully?

With the addition of Lauren, we were now able to track and supplement our lead streams from our Met database. Lauren spent some time analyzing different CRM's and ultimately decided on a particular one because of its ease of use. Although we have had to get used to using something consistently, it's been a great tool for us. Now, we experience about a 9% conversion rate on an annual basis for contacts that know us, utilizing a consistent lead generation system.

We also supplemented what we were doing by purchasing priority presence on Zillow for a particular zip code. We track the number of contacts coming in as well as the conversion rates and gross commission income resulting from leads generated from using this system. At the end of the year we'll figure out our ROI and make future decisions on continuing with that or any other system. Caveat: But please remember, any system we implement doesn't take the place of good old fashioned calling our database. Nothing replaces that. These other systems I mentioned are only suggested to supplement your basic lead generation, if you have leverage to implement and the financial resources to pay for it.

We have created a house warming party system for our new

buyers, as well. 90 days after our clients move to their new home and get settled, we send invitations to their close friends as well as new neighbors. By sending out the invitations, we add contacts to our database. During the Buyer Consultation, we let them know that this is something we do and remind them, throughout the home buying process what fun it will be to entertain friends and family when they finally settle on the right home. Typically, their lender wants to participate in sharing the expenses of the party. The goodwill this party elicits is priceless.

Lastly, I have made it a discipline to build a large referral network with real estate agents around the country and world. The size of the Keller Williams International offers my team a real advantage when meeting other agents at conventions and masterminds. Routinely, I call my referral database as part of my prospecting. Referrals are a large part of my business. When I receive a referral, whether it closes or not, we send Shari's Berries as a thank you to their office. When the berries arrive, other people want to know who sent them and my referral partner tells them, "Sarah Chatel, my referral partner in Atlanta,"

What are the mistakes you have seen leaders make that stifle the growth of their teams?

There are certainly a number of things that leaders can do to stifle the growth of their teams. First, leaders can fail to establish effective systems, choosing to rely on the momentum of a good market and believe that the momentum will last forever. We all know the market is capricious and has its ups and downs. When leaders fail to implement effective systems before any market shift, their business will then, follow the market, up and down. When systems are in place, there is less movement because no matter what the market does, people still need to buy and sell Real Estate. By having consistent systems, people will tend to think of you when they need to make a move, no matter what the market is doing.

Second, leaders can make poor hiring decisions in an attempt to grow the team and business, too fast. At a recent training class on how to hire the right people, the instructor, Ben Kinney, Keller Williams Bellingham, WA., said, "A poor hiring decision can negatively impact the performance of everyone on the team and have a devastating impact on the growth of the team as well as cost you upwards of one million dollars in long term damages." WOW! That got my attention. We now follow a disciplined process for recruiting and selecting new team members. This process includes: personality profile and work behaviors assessments, interviews with other team members, and thorough reference checks. Before anyone is added to the team, we review and consider the input of other team members before making a decision. Where others are not in full support of the candidate, then we proceed cautiously.

When hiring new talent, we "date" them for 90 days to see if they will be a good fit for us. We tell them this up front and let them know that if they aren't a good fit for us we will help them find the right placement as a solo agent or refer them to another team. We are in the business of helping people with their real estate needs, and also to help our team members reach their personal and professional goals.

What resources would you recommend, based on your expertise, that every real estate agent should have?

I'll start with the basics, in terms of resources every real estate agent starting off in the business must have: a computer, contact database of at least 100 people, business cards, name tags with title and business name, a car that is clean and fit for driving clients to appointments, for sale and open house signs, riders, and at least 2 lock boxes. Beyond these basics, I recommend that every new real estate agent obtain a copy and read, Gary Keller's book, *The Millionaire Real Estate Agent*. This is a book that should be read over and over to gain full immersion and referred to continually. It's on my desk with tabs and highlighted for quick reference. Other books, which are required reading for my team, are *The Go-Giver by Bob Berg, 7L – Going from Relationships to Referrals by Michael Maher, Strengths Finders by Tom Rath*. My team does a book club and masterminds around taking one new thing from each thing we read. Beyond these hard items, people starting off in the business must have clear goals, grit to persevere through the challenges they will confront and humility to ask for help when they need it.

Finally, and this is a big thing, a new real estate agent should have at least six months of living expenses available to fund the start-up of their business just in case they don't sell anything that first six months. It does take some time to ramp up, however I've seen agents leap into massive success because of how willing they are to commit to their lead generation and systems set up.

Beyond these basics, I recommend the following resources: a mastermind group with other professionals who are at similar stages of their business to bounce ideas and solicit input, a business coach who can increase self-awareness and drive greater accountability to realize goals, or an accountability partner if you don't have a business coach. Take any and all real estate classes offered, stay learning based. Further, I recommend that agents join groups (e.g., Rotary, Toastmasters, charities of their choice, etc.) where they can network and increase their contact database. Remember, wherever you decide to invest your time to build your network and leads, focus first on delivering value to others by coming from contribution. You will become a magnet for referrals in no time!

Share anything that you would like the readers to know about you and/or your business.

The Distinctive Atlanta Homes (DAH) Team is dedicated to simplifying the business of real estate by leveraging our connections and insights with compassion and integrity in service to others. Our vision is **BOLD INTENTIONAL GROWTH – BIG.** We **think BIG ... act BIG ... achieve BIG.** DAH provides proof that exceeding personal limitations is possible through the power of team. In 2016, we established a *50/50 Goal* – we will help 50 families with their real estate transactions and donate $50,000 to Give Back Homes so that someone will experience the joy of home ownership who otherwise would not have.

We use the following core values and valued behaviors to guide our decision-making and relationships with others.

- **Loyalty** – unwavering devotion and support to our clients
  - ✓ We consistently work for the highest interest of our clients.
  - ✓ We are trustworthy in all our interactions with clients, vendors, attorneys and lenders.
  - ✓ We are steadfast in our care and commitment to our clients.

- **Prosperity** – enabling successful and profitable business transactions
  - ✓ We passionately pursue business success which means the highest good to all concerned.
  - ✓ We are good stewards of the resources with which we are entrusted and use them to ensure a profitable and prosperous business.
  - ✓ We use our wealth wisely and are abundant in our thinking.

- **Charity** -- generously supporting others in need
  - ✓ We willingly give time, talents and resources to others in need and expect nothing in return.
  - ✓ We look for and find ways to give time, talents and resources to others in need.
  - ✓ We use our resources to empower others to overcome challenges but not to enable them to remain imprisoned by pass circumstances.

- **Teamwork** – collaboratively supporting each other as we work to achieve our goals
  - ✓ We work for great and lasting things with and through others.
  - ✓ We work with others to accomplish more than we ever thought possible.
  - ✓ We use discipline and commitment to accomplish goals with others and to realize the greatest rewards possible.

- **Integrity** – honest and truthful in our interactions with others.
  - ✓ We express our true selves in our interactions with others.
  - ✓ We are truthful and honest in our relations with others.
  - ✓ We pursue meaningful relationships through authenticity and vulnerability.

- **Global View** – using a whole world perspective across our business
  - ✓ We think globally but act locally.
  - ✓ We monitor global events and trends and leverage our global connections to benefit our business partners.
  - ✓ We appreciate the differences that exist around the world and the insights that are offered through those differences.

ABOUT SARAH CHATEL

Sarah is a Realtor with Keller Williams, member of KW Global Property Specialist, a lifetime member of the Atlanta Board of Realtors Multi-Million Dollar Sales Club, Certified Luxury Homes Marketing Specialist-Million Dollar Guild recognition, Who's Who in Luxury Real Estate & GPP (Georgia Production Partnership). She and her team, Distinctive Atlanta Homes, work closely with Atlanta Habitat through Give Back Homes, as their charity of choice pledging $50,000 in 2016.

Sarah lives in Virginia Highlands with her husband and two dogs. They have a blended family of five, ages 23 – 29. She and her husband, Peter, are active in the non-for-profit community, their church and Sarah is an active alumnae of Converse College, her alma mater.

Contact:
- Email: contact@distinctiveatlantahomes.com
- Phone: 404-784-4871
- Website: www.distinctiveatlantahomes.com

No matter what people tell you,
words and ideas can change the
world.

Robin Williams